Kazoo Symphonies

~ Beth Wood ~

MEZCALITA PRESS, LLC
Norman, OK

FIRST EDITION, 2015
Copyright © 2015 by Beth Wood
All Rights Reserved.

ISBN-13: 978-0-9837383-5-0

Library of Congress Control Number: 2015912278

No part of this book may be performed, recorded, or otherwise transmitted without the written consent of the author and the permission of the publisher. However, portions of poems may be cited for book reviews—favorable or otherwise—without obtaining consent.

Cover Design: Chris Everett
Front Cover Image: Stock photo © Nikkolia
Back Cover Photo: Cassy Berry

MEZCALITA PRESS, LLC
Norman, Oklahoma

Kazoo Symphonies

~ Beth Wood ~

Table of Contents

Acknowledgements vi

1 – *Water Poems*
I – Anything 5
II – The Princess Ship 6
III – The Story 7
IV – I Get Small 9
V – The Manatee Blues 10
VI – The Deep 11

2 – *Nature Girl*
Grace 15
New Year's Day 16
Nature Girl 17
The Elbow-Shaped Tree in My Front Yard
    and Why I Cannot Love You 18
Birds of Las Vegas 19
Running with Gunner 20
Sentinel Secret 21
Remembering in the Park, No Day in Particular 22
The Secret 23
When I See You (My Gem) 25

3 – *Kazoo Symphonies*
The Piano of My Childhood 29
Here Goes the Flag 30
My Black Friend Trina 32
My Long Tall Skinny Friend the Bull-Rider 34
The Doves 36
Calvin's Song (Most Angels) 38
For Gentle Thunder on Her Birthday 40
Tonto, Revisited 41
Miss Calypso 43

The Wrong Taxi 44
Money 45

4 – Talking Sideways
Favorite Mug 49
Give Me a Poet 50
The Book and the Cover 51
Morning Wonder 52
Some Mornings 53
The Poet's Visit 54
Solid Ground 55
The Word Collector 56
Call It Like It Is 57
Alright, All Right 58

5 – Being Human
Don't Be Afraid, ... 63
Tenderness 64
Only Sunday 66
A Weird Night 67
The Open Window 68
True Love Poem 69
Marriage 70
Home Theatre 71
Fight or Flight 72
Otherwise 73
On Losing 74
Being Human 75
No White Horse 76
The Debt 77

Author Bio 79

Acknowledgements

The unfolding of a poem is one of my favorite things about being alive.

So many Masters have contributed to my deepening love of the mystery…Pablo Neruda, Billy Collins, Mary Oliver, Alicia Ostriker, Nikki Giovanni, Glenis Redmond, Stephen Dunn, E. E. Cummings, Joni Mitchell, and many more.

So many have participated in actively encouraging my writing. I am particularly thankful to poet-friends Jim Chastain and Nathan Brown for inspiration, friendship, laughter, and encouragement.

Thank you to Ashley, Nub and Mezcalita Press, to Chris Everett, and Bob Wood for helping to shape this book into something real. I am ever thankful to my dear ones for cheering me on.

And to you reading this now, I thank you.

~ Beth Wood ~

Kazoo Symphonies

1

Water Poems

I – ANYTHING

If you could do anything, for example float out over this water, then dive into its clear depths without the need for air, dancing a crystalline surrender-dance of melting into a foreign and weightless world, would you? Or you might prefer the comfort of dreaming, the white noise of longing saddled between your ears, humming along and lulling you to sleep through the years upon years upon years. Then one day you wake up with the taste of salt on your mouth, starfish in your hair, singing siren songs under your seaweed breath and you realize, oh this. I could have had it all along.

II – The Princess Ship

From this airplane window I marvel
at light-ribbons on dark water

I observe the hustle and bustle,
the human enterprise of business (busy-ness),
the here and there and there of
manic movement

Parked at the dock sits a handful of runty tugboats—
no glamour, no silver, no sail—
simply waiting patiently with
A Job To Do

It takes a sometimes-fleeting humility to see
that I am not, in fact,
the Princess Ship, but instead
the steady little tugboat bringing her along

full of rust and muscle and heart, chugging
precious cargo—that
shiny something I'll carry with me
until I'm gone.

III – The Story

He loves to tell the story
of our first time snorkeling together
off the coast of Key West
before we had eaten the best meal
of our lives at a tiny place called
Seven Fish (tucked away in a neighborhood),
after the resort we found on the internet
failed to live up to expectation,
after we laughed it off and found the
banana hands growing upside down
right outside our door.
It was before the dolphins swam
right beside our sailboat,
the couple who owned the boat
telling us it's cruel to make dolphins swim
with humans, to lock them away in tanks,
when in fact their curiosity will win every time
if you just let it.
He said no matter what you do,
don't scream or thrash around, that's
how the sharks find you, they'll think you're
prey, like an injured seal bobbling on top
trying desperately to get back to land.
I said okay, I got it, duh.
Then I dipped my head under the dark water,
this alien world, my breath a rhythmic fuzz inside
my head, steady and slow and deep.

First thing I saw with my new eyes was
a shark, a shadow ghost hovering on the ocean floor
right beneath us, his tail sweeping back and forth
like a grey metronome of death. Naturally
I screamed and thrashed and bobbled like a girl
from the plains, I simply couldn't help myself.
He said Baby, gaaaaaawd, what the hell?
and then laughed.
I swam back to the boat and found my breath,
watched the backs of his legs as he floated calmly
and bravely with colorful fish,
and dreamed of a neighborhood restaurant.

IV – I Get Small

I get small
next to you
that's the whole point I think
just like the mountains
I feel a wide expanse
outside myself
a sense of grandeur
watching your cascading waves
and I'm tempted to use words like
majesty, eternity, expansiveness,
infinity—
there I've done it.
it's what I do
when I'm next to you
I get small

V – The Manatee Blues

At the Dallas Aquarium we ran into an intern whose job was to monitor and record the behavior of the manatee (their star attraction) for four-hour shifts. The kid had a clipboard and a sheet of paper with a grid, a box to fill in for every five-minute interval. We asked him if we could read his notes. He said sure. They went like this:

Looping   Looping   Looping   Looping   Looping

Looping   Looping   Looping   Looping   Looping

Looping   Looping   Looping   Looping   Looping

Looping   Looping   Looping   Looping   Looping

I still think about that manatee sometimes
and wonder what he's up to.

VI – The Deep

Some things will remain a mystery,
thank god.
Some things we will never know,

never see, never touch.
You are the last frontier—the unexplored,
the unknowable.

We need you to dream on, to humble us yet again.
Don't you get it? We need you.
To salt-wash us clean of our ambition, our folly—

apologies if we offend.
Of course dead silence is your answer, it's
the answer we've been waiting for.

② Nature Girl

Grace

I guess now I'm old, my idea
of a good time is watching ducks—
the shoveler, merganser, cinnamon teal,
widgeon as they dip and glide, dip
and dive over this glassy water, this
serene scene. Suddenly a pair upset
by geese decides to take flight

tip-tip-toeing and tap-dancing, then
flapping for a few hundred yards before
clumsily crashing down again, goodgod
I love it when they fly

so awkward and unbalanced
so unsure with the landing gear
and then suddenly, they are down again
gliding, leaving whispers of wake behind
in gray waters

makes me think of grace
how every time you manage to find it
you stumble your way in

New Year's Day

I am not the antelope
whose staccato steps quicken
at any sound, her very skin
etched with electricity and dust

Nor am I the kingfisher
shaped like a blade
made to slice the surface
of the deep and take his prey
in an instant

You would think by now
I could say what I am

Instead I walk through this fog
shapeless in the unfolding
New Year's Day
and I wonder how to tell you
what I am lonely for
and why I can't name it

I suppose any explanation
would do, but I can't find one
I stumble and I wait, I
muddle through in wonder,

what's one more year in
the scheme of things

Nature Girl

It should seem obvious that we are not
meant for screens and strange chairs designed
to help our bodies forget that we are sitting
alldamnday. It should be downright glaring
how much more at ease, more fluid my body

might be if it accepted the invitation to sit
in the grass, under the tree, right by the
bright red flower that still surprises me every
year, on a blanket next to the fallingdownfence

that I swear we are going to get fixed
very soon. How hilarious that I am not
there now. But instead I'm in this tiny room
bathed in filtered sunshine, breathing filtered

air, missing what it smells like to be home.
What a riot. A downright rollontheground
laughing fit, good grief. Then why are there
tears and remind me again, when do they stop

THE ELBOW-SHAPED TREE IN MY FRONT YARD AND WHY I CANNOT LOVE YOU

Time walks in funny-shaped lines.
The elbow-shaped tree in my front yard
told me this, laughing
at my brutish naiveté.
Once, years ago I presume,
some kind of cancer ate a hole
in its upward progress.
Detoured, shaken, it still grew
askew, twisted: curved
where it should have been straight,
bold and out of necessity.
Into this face I place your eyes
and they are wet stones.
This is why I cannot love you.

Birds of Las Vegas

Here in this desert mirage,
all seems to shimmer on the horizon:
the raucous shouting lights, the stifling heat pressing
down and rising up, the tourists
from middle America wearing, lets face it,
not enough clothing

you almost can't believe this place

down by the gargantuan pool
you fall asleep in the shade
and wake to birds singing above
your head, it feels
like a half-asleep dream

how could there possibly be birds
in this hellhole? you think to yourself,
just then looking up to the palm tree above you
and seeing three perfect little dusty songbirds
lined up, singing to each other joyfully, without
reserve, the song like lace so delicate

you think of the Bob Marley song and realize
every little thing *will* be alright, just
probably not how you imagined it

Running with Gunner

Body packed full of dynamite,
you have initiated me to these Kansas
dirtroads, darting ahead then stopping
to look back...

*I-thought-we-were-***RUNNING***?,* your
electric amber eyes shout, ***GEEZ!***

Meanwhile I'm plodding the way I do,
marveling at the goldenwheat, the old
leaningbarn, the painted kestrel's hunterprey
ballet, the bunnies you root out and
mercilessly chase, and then suddenly
let go. And by the way,

what happens in you
in that fractured split second
when you decide to let them go?
Something is laughing in your eyes,
some joy-lit fire that shines
for both of us.

And thanks again for leading
me home, I always knew
you would.

Sentinel Secret

I visit the osprey daily now
now that you are gone
she was here before of course
that's how I know her

This world after you so alien—like the math
is off, the lines don't intersect. She stares
straight ahead, her flinty eyes
reminding me it's all just a trick

Her nest a tangled symmetry,
she guards it like a sentinel
(how we marveled when we first saw her)
she raises her wings in the wind,

takes a shit—quite majestically I might add—
and says there's a secret, little one
come back tomorrow
I'll tell you then

REMEMBERING IN THE PARK, NO DAY IN PARTICULAR

What I wouldn't give to
have him back now
his big wet nose sparkling
in the sun, the weight
of his brown body almost
as heavy as mine parked
haphazardly on my foot,
the feeling slowly
leaving my toes but I don't care,
his tail wagging uncontrollably
when I say his name
or say anything for that matter
as I look in his direction
his gentle, sweet, sensitive soul
crowding right up next to mine
while we breathe in and out,
in and out, the children
at the park bathed in sunshine
running after butterflies that fly away
just in the nick of time

The Secret

is an anchor and a balloon.
the secret is a warm blanket,
the wicker chair,
backyard bird-noise,
your favorite sweatshirt,
a ceramic mug,
and the laundry on the line

the secret is the days you spent as a kid riding bikes
patrolling the neighborhood for pirates,
the hike to the top of a mountain at sunrise,
the look on your mother's face when you showed
someone kindness,
the time on the bus when you made a friend

the secret is the day you wet your pants at school,
the lover who couldn't ever really see you,
the things you are sorry for,
your temper tantrum in the car,
and every time you failed to see your own cruelty
even though your bones knew

the secret is the alarm
that woke up the farmer
that planted the grass
that fed the cow
that gave the milk
you poured into your cereal bowl this morning

the secret is the glass half empty
next to the glass half full
and what it takes to change
from one to another

the secret is wonder, grace, bliss, sorrow,
grief, bewilderment, joy

the secret is the song and dance,
your father's hands,
the scars you wear,
and the shouting spring flowers,
the multitude of blessings
that brought you here,
now,
to this town,
this room,
this breath

the secret is this breath
this one tiny breath
it is the engine and the spark,
the anchor and the balloon,
the ten-ton stone and the red-tailed hawk.
it's the only breath you know belongs to you,
it's the only one you know you'll ever get

When I See You (My Gem)

Take me to bogs
and willows, you
can drop me off there

I will pack a sandwich,
stay all day with
winging warblers,

whispering wind. Let
me wade through dark
mud, its old-man gums

sucking my boots until
I'm pulled under, birthing
me new again out of for-

giving earth. A sigh by
the river. Fish listening (they
have ears you know), wait-

ing for one bright incan-
descent wing, deciding it's too
hot after all for turning over,

sun on my shoulders, sky
a slow movie with no plot
and no credits, tall

grass already gone gold,
the day wasted by a stream
all I ever wanted,

my shining gem I
will place in my teeth
for when I see you next

③ Kazoo Symphonies

The Piano of My Childhood

You, standing in the corner—
latent engine,
elephantine angel,
untouched and dust-silent
as a forgotten photo…

here I am passing you
day after day
on my way to the sink,
to my breakfast, to sip coffee,
back to the office, to
bring in the mail

still you never make a sound.

It's not like we took a marriage vow?
(get off my back already)

I told you once—
I don't think of you that way anymore

yet here I am in the half-light
dreaming backwards.

Truth is I broke my heart up against
the stone wall of perfection once.
(stop *bossing* me!)
An optimist could love again.

Here Goes the Flag

Some daddys get scared,
some daddys just don't care,
my Daddy stayed.

I never did know the back
of his hand, or if he
had a war inside,

my Daddy stayed.

In the hospital my Daddy peered over the
machine with the tubes and the
beeps and wondered what on
godsgreenearth to do,

my Daddy stayed.

He let the poison in his veins
so the cancer would not win,

my Daddy stayed.

My Daddy never went to Africa
but he drew a cheetah, a zebra,
a gazelle, made our eyes to wonder,

my Daddy never did climb
to the ladder top,

my Daddy stayed.

My Daddy cried when I wrote
a song, wondered who is this
tender little alien creature?

My Daddy cried when his Daddy
died and he reached out his hand
for me, my favorite gift of all

my Daddy stayed.

That kind of courage never
makes the newspapers, the
shadow-loving TV, no one ever
will raise a flag

so I'm doing it now with
all my might, it's
flying high, so high on a greengold
hill for all the daddys that stay
and that's the Why

cuz my Daddy stayed,
my Daddy stayed, it's
flying so high

my Daddy stayed.

My Black Friend Trina

my black friend Trina
god, what a trip
she cracked me up 'til
my sides hurt y'all

one night in a
toothpaste fight
she called me "shitball"
and we laughed our
asses off right there
on the floor

so I called her that too
and I came home and said

my black friend Trina
god, what a trip
I call her "shitball"!

and BOOM. here comes that curious look.

noooo, don't be stupid,
it's not meant *that* way—
we just had a toothpaste fight
one night and…

my black friend Trina
we made her a gum sculpture

and sent it to her in the mail
cause she said god that's
gross, y'all

my black friend Trina
introduced me to power
without ever having
named it

her voice rang from the rafters
and no one dared
to breathe
she held us in her palms
full of invisible rain

she sang that sometimes she felt
like a motherless child
well I met her Mama twice
but I still believed

she showed me the power
god, what a trip
my black friend Trina

My Long Tall Skinny Friend the Bull-Rider

went down to florida to see a guru
—a guru?—I said and he said yeah

apparently she was an overweight Jewish housewife
when she got—the calling—
started hearing voices thought she was losing it shut herself
in the bathroom (the only room with a lock) her Italian-
stud husband pronounced her CRAZY not to mention
unresponsive-to-her-family's-needs but Jesus said on his
fourth visit when he came down off the cross

—open.—

and she did—

flowerlike, a drawbridge.

she said—hmmmm…okay…I can do this—
they told her buy some land take on
some students give of
yourself to the dying give
lift to their spirits give
love give
presence.

and so she gives
to the dying to AIDS babies that no one

wants cause their little fingernails might
scratch you and their faces sink into death

so my long tall skinny friend the bull-rider
wants to be her student she
gave him a name, he says, which is
an honor.
people say—grumblegrumble, huh, are you CRAZY??—

now I stare at this field of paper and wonder
what is so CRAZY about giving what is so CRAZY
about saying
—i will learn.—

in any case i'll be there to tighten the girth on his saddle
as he rides off into the sunset my long tall
skinny friend the bull-rider i'll be there to say
—nighthorse, carry him well—

but oops, silly me!
bull-riders don't need saddles.
and nighthorses ride along fences faithfully
regardless of words.

—a nighthorse??—you say and we both say
yeah.

The Doves

Helicopter Man
with cigarette hands, huge
gold-rimmed tinted glasses and a
seventies mustache
tall and slight, but not sunken in—
so exotic to this dutiful
suburban girl

Singapore and Tehran,
Columbia, Mexico, Taiwan
and Vietnam

And yet you returned to the tiny little
Texas town that broke you in

to scorpions and rusted tractor
pieces strewn all about, to the Friday night
Elks Club and snake-bit dogs,
to your grandfather's grocery

who never had the heart to
let anyone go hungry

Perhaps his memory fed you
starved out there from the years of
running from your father's fists,
his poison words

Once I went along with you
dove-hunting, my tender heart splitting
open when you wrung their little
necks, blood showering your jeans,
the ground, your manner never mean
just matter-of-fact as I
shivered there in the heat

but you were proud of me anyway
you said, patting me on the head, a single
grey feather in my hand

Well you can rest now, it's done
there's nothing more to run from
her arms are waiting, the doves
have all bled out

Calvin's Song (Most Angels)

I'll never forget Calvin Drumgold.
I can still see his name *Calvin* in cursive
on his chest

It could have been his casual kindness
or his tough-guy strut

Or maybe it was the way he said *Damn, girl!*
when I sang for him in the parking lot,
jumping back like he had touched a hot coal

It could have been his beautiful cornrows that I
longed to touch, to graze my fingers across their
rugged symmetry, dying to know how long it took
to get them in and did it hurt

But most likely it was the way he navigated the intersection
of two colliding principles: Shit Happens, and
It's Hard to Watch A Baby Bird Struggle.

Hey Calvin, the man-who-was-in-charge shouted,
you off your shift?

Yeah, Calvin said.

Can you help this little girl change a flat?

Ahhhhh, sure, Calvin said,
no beat missed,
his shoulders sinking in to the reality
of his next twenty minutes

You play that thing? he asked, eyeing my guitar case
as we walked together in the Georgia heat.
Yes, I said, raw and embarrassed at needing help
And when the deed was done, and I tried clumsily
to repay his time and sweat and kindness with
a folded up bill, he said *Naaaah.*
Just sing one for me and we're cool.

He probably doesn't know it,
Calvin Drumgold,
how I'll never ever forget

Most angels never do.

For Gentle Thunder on Her Birthday

Gentle thunder
rolling through the hills
bringing in the summer
rain, calling me
out to play, to joy

you rumble beneath
the surface, finding
ways to shake the world
(you are thunder
after all)

I am just a farmer
planting seeds, crumpled
map of heart in hand
wondering, how did
I get here?

and how did you know
this would be the time
for rolling out rain? You just
know. That's the
gentle part.

Tonto, Revisited

See the shaggy
   white pony in the photo
his mane standing up Mohawk style
   his jagged hooves unshorn

oh how he saved
   that little girl next to him
the one with the green puffy coat
   and the fake fur hood
and the shiny purple eyeshadow from
   playing cousin dress-up

how he took her into the brightday
   annoyed and amused by this little pest
who came with oats, brushes, songs,
   whispered words

continually playing the game of
   how-to-scrape-her-off be it tree
or barn or hot rock

   but how they sailed alone together
wind in their hair, empty fields
   of grass in the wind, away from that stone
house of murmurs and tears and heavy
   unnamed grief.

In the corner of my closed eyes
   I can see him now—proud and tall
like he just rolled in dirt, he's
   standing like an exclamation point

alone there on the prairie.
   Well I'll be damned. I think
he has come for me this time.

Miss Calypso

There is a light in the world
called Maya Angelou
that cannot be extinguished
or even dimmed
but burns bright as ever,
same as the sun

There was a child
who so fiercely objected to
injustice that she stopped
all speaking. The words
grew there in her head,
she let the dough rise
a good long time until
it was ready

Then she sang and sang and
never stopped singing the song
for her heart, for all of our
hearts before she knew it.
Everyday she sings a song
that sounds like the light
of the world. Miss Calypso,
bright bird, flown now but
hardly gone.

The Wrong Taxi
(for RLJ)

If you reached out your
wrinkled mother's hand into me
then I would have no fear of what I saw
behind my eyes
echoing you
echoing you

your woman's body flailing at pretense
and stomping it to the ground
your calloused old fingers grabbing at chords
    you shriek
    you lean back
    you clench your fists and growl
    —come ON, boys—
your wild braids dancing
like paintbrushes in the night air

This
is what I am here for
This
is why I am here
This
is my reason I was missing
one more chapter or verse

because you reached out your wrinkled mother's
hand into me

and squeezed with all your might.

Money

What will you be when you grow up? the teacher asks
hopefully of her young students, their hands shooting
up in the air like tiny rocketships, pick me, pick me!—

a nurse, a fireman, a president, a reporter,
an actress, a doctor, a veterinarian. What
will you do to get money? she never asks

because when it comes down to brass tacks, we
need money to survive, apparently, in this
ghostworld we have closed our eyes and dreamed.

I didn't know to separate the two—a gullible
kid, head in the clouds, busy writing kazoo
symphonies in my mind during economics class.

It comes and it goes like the weather or like a breath.
Last month was a good one, even prosperous you might
say, yet there is the envelope next to the letter from

the food pantry kitchen. In the paper is the fundraising
effort for the girl who was beaten to death by her fiancé
with a baseball bat, she was an equestrian, she has

five horses to feed, whose hunger carries on in a
straight line after the curvature of her death. And
there is, of course, always public radio. It just

comes and it goes and I sigh, letting go of breath.
And that's the way, if I'm being honest,
I've come to like it.

Talking Sideways

Favorite Mug

I try not to love *things*
but sometimes it simply cannot be helped.
My fuzzy robe, Grandfather's green pitcher,
this favorite coffee mug, imperfect and lopsided
and hand-made. I've tried drinking from others
but it's never the same, never as good.
Furthermore, for quite some time I have ignored
all sentences that contain the words 'supposed to',
never quite satisfied with the mystery of who
is doing all the supposing. So I'm all alone here again
now with my mug in a blank field, the trees dissolving
to white, wishing for just a moment I could be
someone else, that way I could be doing
all of the supposing.

Give Me a Poet

Give me a poet in dangerous times—
our most powerful ammunition,
their words seeping in with the slow urgency
of seabound snow-melt. Think
of all the ones who were murdered,
exiled, tortured, body and
soul sundered for all time

the bitter aftertaste being that
you cannot stop a voice

Think of the ones who have died
for truth, the inescapable beauty
of illusion winging them to another world
with all the words they have never spoken,
all the faces of hope, the pitifully
ironic glow of warm sunrise
on a battlefield

The Book and the Cover

The book and the cover.

The cover and the book.

The message in the book.

The message in the cover.

The budget for the book.

The budget for the cover.

The kid who piles too much food on his plate

because his eyes are hungry.

The kid who is hungry.

The price of ambition.

The price of art.

The price of the book.

And the cover.

The cost.

Morning Wonder

This is the cup
that I pour my coffee into,
this is the table where I
place my chair.
this is the too-dark coffee that shouts,
"I am too dark,"
this is my belly being warmed
inch by inch.
this is the window that I
stare out of,
these are the things
that I wonder.
these are the words
that I write, in a list.
those are the sounds
of the morning birds,
there is the lizard
warming in the new sun,
this is the ritual of
the morning.

these are the hurtful things I carry
(that I picked up along the way).
this is me as I see them.
this is how I wonder
at how you love me,
this is how they melt away.

Some Mornings

Some mornings you stare at the blank page blankly

actually, most mornings

actually, all mornings.

Sometimes minute things emerge in the stillness
like evergreen buds in this rain-soaked soil—
remnants of a dream you squint to remember,
the memory of a childhood laugh shared with siblings
in a tree, back in the time before heartsick,
before grief

Sometimes, quite surprised, you find a ball of clay
in your hands and you simply knead
with your eyes closed—
a quiet victory taking shape,
a quiet Joy

Then again sometimes you can't find the clay

Sometimes you can't quite find
the morning,
your hands,
the page

The Poet's Visit

Oh my beautiful city
where the river cuts through,
where bright autumn leaves are glued by rain
to the sidewalk, where we cherish our
wild places but not always
wild things, where one December night
a war veteran and animal lover
froze to death in the gutter with
vodka by his side,

the Famous Poet comes in three days.

Take him to our nicest places, let him
marvel and sigh at the view from the butte,
feed him artful and wonder-filled things, wine
from our fields, abundance from our
rich earth. Tell him we are proud,

so proud, but we're
ashamed at the same time.

He'll know what to do

Solid Ground

The worst you can do
for heavensakes is be earnest
declared the ironic artist

from his disheveled lectern,
glasses perching on the tip of his nose
like a plastic bird about to fly,

weird symmetrical patches of hair
growing up the sides of his
otherwise bald canvas of head.

Maybe that's my problem
I think to myself, as if he is
speaking directly to me, the only

slightly earnest poetgirl in the room.
Or maybe it's that I think everyone *else*
is earnest, taking them at face value,

never imagining they are talking
sideways. Me on a wire. The
others dancing a double-time jig

and never second guessing a thing.

The Word Collector

The writer says to collect the words.

How wonderful to find a fellow collector!

I always fancied myself their steward,
a foster parent in charge
of guiding them safely along
until the parting comes.
I protect them,
adore them,
secretly have my favorites.
I am haunted by several,
how they have been used, abused,
mistreated.

I am baffled at how they all exist at the same time,
like numbers. How can there possibly be
so much space?

I smile a crooked spring smile.
The children are coming,
they are never ours to keep.

Call It Like It Is

This is called morning
it happens everyday
the curtain opens and we
begin again

bright, fuzzy,
soaked in rain
each one a different
little snowflake

The remembering
is the hard part,
every day the gift
erased,

and forgetting
so easy I'm beginning
to suspect we need
an intervention

or at least a swift
kick in the ass, and
then we'll call it
a day.

Alright, All Right

If there is a blank field
that's alright
your life is a blank field

If there is silence
that's alright
everything begins from silence as it ends there

If there is never enough
that's alright
enough is there, it's just hiding

If there is pacing back and forth
that's alright
a cage will do that after all

If there is little faith
that's alright
faith is its own engine, its own fuel

If there is fear
that's alright
fear is the place where speed comes from

If there are doubts
that's alright
that's the old man shielding the child from rain

If there is a pattern to this all
that's alright
it's just beautiful geometry

And if there is beautiful geometry
that's alright—
a simple kindness that says: it's all right.

5

Being Human

Don't Be Afraid,

she always says. As if it were that easy, as if everything were smooth sailing, falling slowly, never worrying about the ground below.

The sound of the hammer on a nail, the metal to the bone, the wall of graffiti, the unmistakable feeling that you have forgotten something.

Something borrowed or blue or coming unglued, something from no-thing, the underside of what is true, the dark behind the light, the seamless stream of days like an endless flowing river, the forgotten time and place, the face of someone who stole your heart, a heart that sinks like a stone to the bottom of the sea. Shoreline to the left, mountains to the right, birds hovering above my head.

Don't be afraid, always ringing false in my head, like saying don't be blue to the sky, don't be wet to water. Follow what is true and you will all-ways be surprised at what you have found, I say while you are afraid you will find beauty there in the stones, a gift back from the sea to hold in your hand forever.

Tenderness

It sounds like running water
for a bath—just right, not
too hot—when a woman's hands would
pat you, soap you, tickle
your skin dry

Or like football on television
(back when you had to get up to change the channel)
you asleep on the floor in the crook of your
father's right arm, family dog
asleep in the other

Never is it owed to you, you learn
nor can it be taken
and for the weight of that knowing your
whole body aches

Your grandmother's white-cotton-sheet voice
begging you to sit on her lap so she could
rock you, rock you, rock you sweet child

Once in the kitchen she leaned in
to whisper, said there was sugar behind your ear
and you shrugged up your shoulder in reflex,
her breath fluttering goosefeathers on
your neck

"I love you, I love you, I love you," she whispered

up close, but you thought she said
"coffee, coffee, coffee" and that was
forever and always
the running joke between you

You know it's coming on like weather, but
the phone call enters when the lights
are already out, heavy black night pressing
you down into the bed so you can't get up

Not with the school-book kind of knowing
but with the deep-down kind:
she cannot hold you now

You will never hear the sound again

Only Sunday

I am walking in a cloud of grief,
   my husband is a bright sparrow.

I cannot stop the tears,
   he sings the day into being.

I worry that he will suffer here,
   grow tired, want to fly,

but a sparrow sings
   because he sings, no?

He smiles at me over the
   morning paper, I

burn my lips with coffee. Smile
   back, Fool, I say to myself,

already unhinged, and it's
   only Sunday

A Weird Night

Good lord, what a weird night.
Our old dog is fading and I am trying to
let go, but in my half-sleep I
forget what to listen for, and
he poops right beside the bed.

I wake up to the smell
and mumble "what the *hell?*"
out loud, fumble in sock-feet
with carpet-cleaners, air-fresheners,
matches and candles, and
oddly enough I find myself
kneeling down and apologizing
to him, his old stiff bones creaking,
the shifting sounds of a quiet
house in the rain lulling
us both back to sleep

while we wait for the flame
to burn out

The Open Window

I know I said it would be strange
but I never imagined it
I knew we would end up here
but it's not on the map
I didn't know what to bring
so I brought nothing. Nothing
but my heartbeat, this pen
and paper, that sigh

Ever Grateful, I keep repeating
like a mantra
like a lifeline

and it's true
I am

even grateful for this day,
this August sun at my back,
these familiar tears and the weight
of grief, the supper waiting
to be made, my hands
fidgeting without the busyness
of you. This open window
you flew out of
and the warm breeze that flew in

True Love Poem

"Is it true love?" they ask
as if all other love is false,
as if we are not at the core
hopeful creatures sorting out
and discarding our unpleasant memories
like weeds in a garden

what is a promise
but a measure of hope?
When in truth I cannot tell you that
in ten years from now I won't
want to tear your head off and drive away
leaving your weeds,
this soil, my garden

but what I do know
with all kinds of certainty
is that I can promise to love

because love does not end
love does not wither and love is not,
in fact, a contract

it can only be a gift, a seed. And you
can only rest on your knees in the dirt,
water-can in hand, and hope
for some return

Marriage

Here we go.
We took it to the mountain and
said Yes
even though we were
already saying it
in here

we have giggled
and danced here all along,
twinned and gap-sealed
and not sure the origin
of this luck

yet still at times it's like walking
with a full cup of coffee, you think
—I'm cruising now—
but careful, C-A-R-E-F-U-L or
you might spill

no harm done if it's mostly full
when you get there

Home Theatre

I had a dream you wrote
a play and we were in it
you said here's the tightrope you walk
now walk it
I said but all these people might see me fall
you said yes they might
and you exited stage left

all the while the band plays pure silence
the drummer does not roll
the weeping ladies in the balcony let their
tears fall below leaving saltmarks
on vintage upholstery

the children grow restless
the lights heave a heavy sigh
my stomach makes animal noises
and I put one foot out
touch the rope, think my balance
just might be found

and then the clowns come in.

Fight or Flight

The Funny Man said to have courage—
it sounds like such a simple thing

That you are Fight and I am Flight remains
like a burr in my shoe. Take for example

the car wreck in front of us that
still lives behind my eyes like a dream.
Me stunned into silence, then running
here and there, throwing the car in
reverse after you had run out to
the overturned van, mother screaming,
sirens coming in slow motion. I wanted
to run, I had to run, but you ran in.

That kind of courage I admire deeply and
from afar like some grand, chaotic painting
I do not understand, that is art
but I don't know why

The Funny Man said think of that kind of courage
and do something—ONE thing you didn't think
you could do. Well when you put it like that it
sounds simple. We can all do one thing. Maybe
for you it's to stay and put your armor down.
Maybe for me it's to run to you.

Otherwise

I have left your pedestal
it's empty now
such a stark sad sight
you perhaps not even remembering
now it was there

and let's be honest
you have left mine

but get real.

we could not have built this
from above
floating in the ether
we would have been something
suspended, something pillowy,
featherly, something
otherwise

now we argue over headphones
and slamming doors
the moment owns us my dear, finally
we have arrived.

On Losing

We sigh at this thing called
loss
we chew on the words
"oh poor thing…"
hanging on to every sumptuous sound,
buzzing in our throats like
a king's mantra

as if just this morning
we didn't swerve to miss an
on-coming truck

as if our tears have no memory—
tiny little soldiers doing their duty
and then disappearing to start
lives of their own

as if our hearts didn't break
just looking at a child,
wondering when the magnificent
halo of light will fade, or
altogether disappear

Being Human

Being human
is loving with
all your heart,
all the while waiting
to see
what next you will lose

No White Horse

There is, most likely,
no white horse

but on the thimble's off chance
that there is, he's
wild as the day he was born,
standing in the distance on top of
the heathered hill, closer
to sky, stamping and snorting
with a crazed look in his eye, just
daring you to not just stand there,
do something.

The Debt

I am in debt to my spirit
I took out a loan and I have not
paid it back
I have mistreated my body, which is
also on loan
I have misused my heart, which belongs
only to me
I have said things to myself that I
would never say to another person,
animal, or (in most cases) even
an inanimate object
I have bought into the hype
I have danced to the wrong music
I have refused to slow down because
stillness hurts
I have looked away
I have taken from others what I could not
give myself
I have bargained with tears

I am human
I want to pay it back.

Author Bio

Beth Wood is a singer-songwriter, poet, modern-day troubadour, and believer in the power of song. Her exceptional musicianship, crafty songwriting, powerful voice, and commanding stage presence have been winning over American audiences for eighteen years.

Beth began her journey in Lubbock, a high plains Texas town with a uniquely rich musical heritage that includes Buddy Holly, Natalie and Lloyd Maines, Mac Davis, and Joe Ely, to name a few. Eighteen years, thousands of shows, nine albums, three cars, and numerous awards later, Beth has never looked back.

Beth has been featured on Oregon Public Broadcasting's *Artbeat* and on *Troubadour, TX*, a nationally syndicated documentary-style singer-songwriter reality television series airing in almost 40 million households and 140 U.S. markets, and her songwriting has been recognized by the Kerrville Folk Festival (New Folk Award), Sisters Folk Festival (Winner of the Dave Carter Memorial Songwriting Contest) and more.

But always in the background, even before the songs, was poetry. Now it is out in the open, and Beth can share her poems with those who love her music, and beyond.

www.ingramcontent.com/pod-product-compliance
Lightning Source LLC
Chambersburg PA
CBHW031208090426
42736CB00009B/830